SPORTS
STARTERS

Slap shot Hockey

John Crossingham

 Crabtree Publishing Company

www.crabtreebooks.com

Created by Bobbie Kalman

Dedicated by John Crossingham
For my daughter Isla, who's kind enough to watch hockey with her daddy.

Author
John Crossingham

Editors
Kelley MacAulay
Adrianna Morganelli
Robert Walker

Photo research
Crystal Sikkens

Design
Margaret Amy Salter

Production coordinator
Katherine Kantor

Illustrations
Trevor Morgan: pages 4, 6, 7, 8, 10, 12, 14, 16, 18, 20, 22, 24, 26, 28, 30

Photographs
Associated Press: pages 18, 27 (bottom)
Marc Crabtree: pages 9 (top), 30
Icon SMI: Shelly Castellano: page 21 (bottom); John Cordes: pages 5, 21 (top), 27 (top); Jerome Davis: page 1; IHA: page 19; Richard C. Lewis: page 29; Andy Mead: pages 8, 15, 24, 25, 26; Bryan Singer: page 28; Ray Stubblebine: page 17; Ed Wolfstein: page 9 (middle); Zuma: pages 9 (bottom), 11 (middle)
iStockphoto.com: pages 3, 11 (top), 31 (bottom)
© 2008 Jupiterimages Corporation: page 11 (bottom)
© Photosport.com: pages 20, 22
Shutterstock.com: back cover, pages 4, 6, 10, 12, 13, 14, 16, 23, 31 (top)
Other images by Photodisc

Library and Archives Canada Cataloguing in Publication

Crossingham, John, 1974-
    Slap shot hockey / John Crossingham.

(Sports starters)
Includes index.
ISBN 978-0-7787-3142-9 (bound).--ISBN 978-0-7787-3174-0 (pbk.)

    1. Hockey--Juvenile literature. I. Title. II. Series: Sports starters
(St. Catharines, Ont.)

GV847.25.C76 2008   j796.962   C2008-900929-0

Library of Congress Cataloging-in-Publication Data

Crossingham, John, 1974-
    Slap shot hockey / John Crossingham.
        p. cm. -- (Sports starters)
    Includes index.
    ISBN-13: 978-0-7787-3142-9 (rlb)
    ISBN-10: 0-7787-3142-1 (rlb)
    ISBN-13: 978-0-7787-3174-0 (pb)
    ISBN-10: 0-7787-3174-X (pb)
    1. Hockey--Juvenile literature. I. Title.
    GV847.25.C76 2008
    796.962--dc22

                          2008004850

Crabtree Publishing Company

www.crabtreebooks.com   1-800-387-7650

Published in Canada
Crabtree Publishing
616 Welland Ave.
St. Catharines, Ontario
L2M 5V6

Published in the United States
Crabtree Publishing
PMB16A
350 Fifth Ave., Suite 3308
New York, NY 10118

Published in the United Kingdom
Crabtree Publishing
White Cross Mills
High Town, Lancaster
LA1 4XS

Published in Australia
Crabtree Publishing
386 Mt. Alexander Rd.
Ascot Vale (Melbourne)
VIC 3032

Contents

What is hockey?

Hockey is one of North America's most popular team sports. In team sports, groups of athletes (teams) play against each other. Hockey is played on a sheet of ice called a **rink**. Players wear **skates** to move on the ice and they use **sticks** to move a small rubber disk called a **puck** .

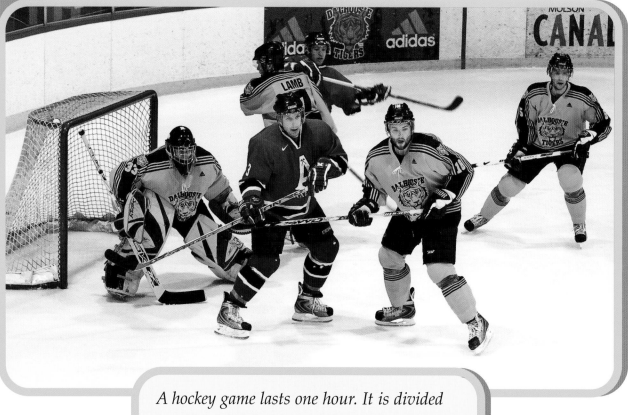

*A hockey game lasts one hour. It is divided into three 20-minute sections called **periods**.*

Shoots and scores!

In hockey, players try to score **goals**. A goal is scored when a player **shoots** the puck into a net. There are two nets in hockey, one for each team to protect, or defend. The team with the most goals wins.

Offense and defense

When a team has the puck and is trying to score, they are playing **offense**. The team trying to stop them from scoring are playing **defense**.

*Each team has five players (and one **goaltender**) on the ice at a time.*

Enter the arena

Most rinks are found inside buildings called **arenas**. The rink is divided in half by a red line. Each team has its own end, or side, which is marked by a blue line.

Places people!

Each player has a position, or job, on the team. There are six hockey positions: goaltender, left and right defense, left and right wing, and **center**. Centers and **wingers** are also called **forwards**. Each position uses different skills to help the team win. Keep reading to learn more about them all!

Face-off!

A hockey game begins with a **face-off** at the center circle. In a face-off, the puck is dropped between each team's center, who try to get the puck to their own teammates. Anytime play stops, a face-off is held at one of the face-off circles found around the rink.

goaltender
(see page 12)

goal line

This is the red team's end. Here they try to keep the yellow team from scoring goals.

defense
(see page 14)

wingers
(see page 18)

red line

center circle

center
(see page 16)

blue line

*High walls called **boards** surround the edge of the rink.*

face-off circle

face-off dot

net

7

Hockey moves

Skating isn't the only skill players must learn in hockey. Using a stick correctly is also very important to playing the game.

*A **body check** is when a defender uses his body to take **opposition** out of the play.*

Passing is an important part of the offense, as well as a good way to keep the puck away from opponents.

A **defenseman** must be able to switch from skating forward to skating backward quickly.

Defenders stop opponents by **checking** them. A **poke check** is when the defender uses his stick to knock the puck away from an opponent.

Shoot it!

One of the most important moves in hockey is the shot. Players use **wrist shots**, **backhand shots**, and **slap shots** to the put the puck in the defender's net.

When shooting, a player must keep his head up and stay focused on where he wants the puck to go.

Sharp shooters

There are three main types of shots in hockey—wrist shots, backhands, and slap shots.

Players perform a wrist shot by flicking their wrists to shoot the puck. These shots are quick and easy to aim.

Players perform a backhand shot by hitting the puck with the back of the stick blade.

stick blade

To perform a slap shot, a player hits the puck as hard as possible. While harder to aim than the wrist shot, the slap shot can move so fast the goaltender can't see it until it's too late.

The goaltender

A goaltender is also called a goalie. A goalie's main job is to stop pucks from entering the net. When a goalie stops a puck, that is called making a save. Goalies always have pucks flying at them! They wear thick pads and facemasks to protect their bodies.

catching glove

blocker

*Goalies use a bigger stick, a **blocker**, and a **catching glove** to make saves.*

Goaltenders take special care to cover as much of the net with their bodies as possible.

Side to side

Goaltenders do not need to skate fast like other players. Instead, they must be able to move from side to side very quickly. Goalies must have flexible bodies so that they can throw themselves easily in front of the puck.

The defense

The left and right defensemen protect their net from offensive attacks. They check opponents and **intercept**, or stop, the other team's passes. Defensemen always try to stay between opponents and the net.

These defensemen are blocking the net. Defensemen also put their stick in the way of the opponent's pass—also known as blocking the passing lane.

Not just defense

The defensemen help their team switch from playing defense to playing offense. When on defense, a player will poke check the puck away from an opposing player. The player must then pass the puck quickly to a forward, who will try to score a goal. Now the team is playing offense!

Get back!

Defenders must be able to turn quickly from skating forward to skating backward. This helps block opponents from reaching the defensive net.

Defensive players often drop to the ice to block a shot by the other team. This defenseman helps his team's goaltender by stopping an opponents' shot.

The center

A center is the player that leads the team when it is playing offense. The center is often the biggest and strongest player on the team. They use their size and strength to block and check players on the other team's defense who are trying to steal the puck.

The center performs the face-off for the team. The center wins the face-off by knocking the puck to a teammate before the opposing center can.

Mats Sundin is one of the NHL's best passers. This big, strong, center makes great passes that allow teammates to score.

The playmakers

A strong center is often called a team's **playmaker**. Playmakers have a lot of **assists**—they pass the puck to set up a teammate to score a goal. Great passes are just as important to hockey as goals.

The wingers

Wingers are usually the fastest players on their team. They are also often the team's **snipers** (great at **aiming** the puck). When a winger is skating toward the net, he aims his shot for the part of the net that the goalie is not blocking. The winger often scores the most points of any player on the team.

Brenden Morrow, left winger for the Dallas Stars, has great aim. Here, Morrow scores a goal against Anaheim Ducks goalie Jean-Sebastien Giguere.

When **deking**, the player with the puck uses stick-work and quick movements to avoid opposing players and hold onto the puck.

Rules and referees

Officials watch over the game to make sure everyone follows the rules. There are two kinds of officials — **referees** and **linesmen**. Referees are the head officials and they are helped by the linesmen. There are two referees and two linesmen at a hockey game.

Hockey officials wear black and white striped uniforms (referees add orange armbands to their outfits).

Offensive blunders

One of hockey's most important rules is **offside**. An offensive player breaks this rule by crossing the other team's blue line before the puck does. The offside rule prevents offensive players from waiting by the other team's net to score a goal.

Icing on the rink

Icing is when a defensive player shoots the puck from his own end of the rink to the other (putting his team on the offensive). If a defensive player reached the puck first, play is stopped and a face-off is held at the opposite end.

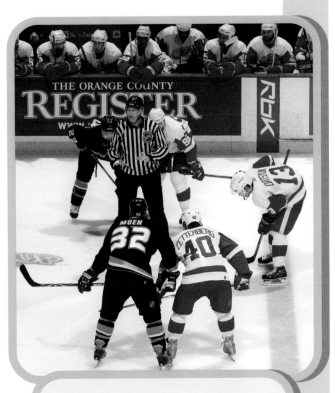

Players cannot cross the blue line into their opponent's end before the puck. If they do, they are offside and play is stopped. A face-off is then held at a dot just outside the blue line.

A referee signals an icing call by raising his arm.

The power play

When a player breaks a rule, the referee will call a **penalty**, sending that player to sit in the **penalty box**. This leaves his team one player short on the ice and gives the opposition a **power play**.

A player who gets a penalty must sit in the penalty box until either the penalty ends or the other team scores.

Special teams

Special teams are the players used during a power play or a penalty. When on a power play, a team will want its best scorers and passers on the ice. Having been given a penalty, a team's strong defensive players are needed to make up for being one player short.

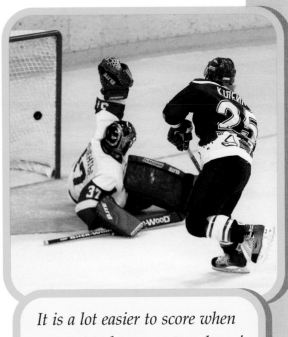

It is a lot easier to score when your team has an extra player!

Penalties

Most penalties that are minor last for two minutes. Minor penalties are given for tripping, **slashing**, or holding an opponent. Major penalties are more serious five-minute penalties. Fighting is a major penalty, receiving five minutes in the penalty box.

Fighting another player puts you in the penalty box!

Shootout!

Sometimes at the end of the third period, the score is **tied** (both teams have the same number of goals). When the score is tied, the game goes into **overtime**, which means the teams play an extra period. Overtime usually lasts for five minutes. The first team to score a point in overtime wins the game.

In overtime, the excitement of a game rises. The saves are bigger, the hits are harder, and the crowd is louder.

Power trio

If neither team can score in overtime, there is a **shootout**. Each side chooses three players for a one-on-one contest with the opposing goaltender. Players only get one chance to score.

It is very exciting when a player wins the game during a shootout!

The NHL

The most popular hockey league in the world is the **NHL** (National Hockey League). Begun in 1917 with only six teams, the NHL has grown to 30 teams across Canada and the United States. The original six teams were Toronto Maple Leafs, Montreal Canadians, Boston Bruins, New York Rangers, Detroit Red Wings, and Chicago Blackhawks.

*The top team of every NHL season is awarded with the **Stanley Cup**.*

The Stanley Cup

Every year the top teams in the NHL compete for the Stanley Cup. Named after former Canadian Governor General Lord Stanley, the cup is awarded to the winner of the NHL **playoffs** held at the end of each season.

Hockey everywhere

The NHL isn't the only popular hockey league in the world. The **AHL** (American Hockey League) has many NHL **farm teams** and draws impressive crowds. European leagues in Sweden, Finland, Norway, Germany, and Russia are known for their exciting hockey and gifted players.

Hockey superstars

Legends like Wayne Gretzky, Bobby Orr and Mario Lemieux have inspired many people to play hockey. Here are some of the greatest young stars in the game today!

Sidney Crosby

Crosby may be the greatest hockey player since Wayne Gretzky. This Pittsburgh Penguins' center earned over 100 points in his first year in the NHL.

Vincent Lecavalier

Quick and strong, Tampa Bay's Lecavalier is one of hockey's most skilled young players. In the 2006-2007 season he scored 52 goals to win the **Maurice Richard trophy** as the NHL's top scorer.

Alexander Ovechkin

This Russian star was picked as the NHL's top **rookie** in the 2005-2006 season. Though new to the league, Ovechkin is already one of the NHL's best scorers.

Roberto Luongo

Everyone has a hard time scoring on Luongo. This Vancouver Canuck made 72 saves in one game against Dallas in 2007.

Dion Phaneuf

Phaneuf is a defenseman for the Calgary Flames. He is loved by fans for his high energy and tough checking style.

Pick up the game

Are you curious about where you can start playing hockey? If you live in a part of North America with cold winters, you can probably find plenty of hockey teams to join. Hockey is even becoming popular in warmer states like California, Florida, and North Carolina.

Hockey equipment can be very expensive. Try to find second hand equipment when starting out.

Schools and gyms

Ask at your school or local sports club about good places to begin learning to play hockey. If you are a first-time skater, be patient. Skating is not like walking or running, but with practice, you can do it!

Listen to coaches as they give you tips on skating, checking, and passing.

Take it to the street

If you can't find any ice, hockey is also a lot of fun to play on pavement. Street hockey can be played on any quiet stretch of concrete. All you need are some friends, sticks for everyone, and a ball (a tennis ball works best). Have fun!

Glossary

Note: Some boldfaced words are defined where they appear in the book.

aim To direct the puck at a certain spot when shooting

blocker A goalie's glove worn on the hand holding the stick; used to deflect the puck

catching glove A goalie's glove used to catch and hold the puck

checking To steal the puck by knocking it away from your opponent with your body or stick

farm team An amateur team where NHL teams develop players

opposition A person on the other team

penalty box A closed in bench at the side of the rink where a player must sit after breaking a rule

playoffs Games played after the regular season to determine the champion team

power play A situation in which one team has more players on the ice because the opposing team has one or more players in the penalty box

rookie A person who is in their first year of playing professional hockey

shoot Striking a puck with the end of the hockey stick

skates Sturdy boots with narrow metal blades attached to the bottom used to travel on ice

slashing Swinging a stick at another player's body

stick A long, narrow piece of wood with a curved end used to move the puck

Index

Printed in the U.S.A.